Pebble

Countries

Kenya

by Christine Juarez

Consulting Editor: Gail Saunders-Smith, PhD

CAPSTONE PRESS
a capstone imprint

Pebble Books are published by Capstone Press,
1710 Roe Crest Drive, North Mankato, Minnesota 56003
www.capstonepub.com

Library of Congress Cataloging-in-Publication Data
Cataloging-in-Publication information is on file with the Library of Congress.
ISBN 978-1-4765-5169-2 (paperback)

Editorial Credits
Erika L. Shores, editor; Bobbie Nuytten, designer; Tracy Cummins, media researcher;
Laura Manthe, production specialist

Photo Credits
Flickr: Mark Skipper, 13; Getty Images: Nigel Pavitt, 11; Newscom: DANIEL IRUNGU/EPA,
15, Sergio Pitamitz/Robert Harding, 19, Stephen Morrison/EPA, 17; Photos.com: Stockbyte,
22; Shutterstock: Andrzej Kubik, 1, Itinerant Lens, 9, Ivsanmas, 4, KA Photography KEVM111,
21, Natalia Pushchina, 5, Ohmega1982, back cover (globe), Oleg_Mit, 22, Paul Banton, cover,
PHOTOCREO/Michal Bednarek, 7, sahua d, cover, 1 (design element)

Note to Parents and Teachers

The Countries set supports national social studies standards related to
people, places, and culture. This book describes and illustrates Kenya. The
images support early readers in understanding the text. The repetition
of words and phrases helps early readers learn new words. This book
also introduces early readers to subject-specific vocabulary words, which
are defined in the Glossary section. Early readers may need assistance to
read some words and to use the Table of Contents, Glossary, Read More,
Internet Sites, and Index sections of the book.

Printed in the United States of America in North Mankato, Minnesota.
092013   007764CGS14

Table of Contents

Where Is Kenya?

Kenya is a country in eastern Africa. It is about the size of the U.S. state of Texas. Kenya's capital is Nairobi.

KENYA

★Nairobi

Landforms

Kenya has many landforms. Beaches line the coast of the Indian Ocean. Savannas and the Chalbi Desert are north of the coasts. Mountains are in the west.

Animals

In Kenya, lions and cheetahs chase antelope across savannas. Hippos cool themselves in muddy rivers. Elephants, zebras, and giraffes also roam Kenya.

Language and Population

Kenya has 44 million people.

Most Kenyans live in the countryside.

Kenyans speak Kiswahili or English.

Other languages are spoken by different groups of native people.

Food

Corn is the main food in Kenya. Ugali is a common dish. It is made of corn flour and water. It becomes a dough that Kenyans eat alongside vegetables or meat.

Celebrations

Kenyans celebrate Jamhuri Day on December 12. It marks the day Kenya became its own country. People enjoy large meals, dancing, and parades.

Where People Work

Most Kenyans are farmers. Coffee beans and tea grow on large farms. Farmers sell these crops for money. On smaller farms, people grow corn to feed their families.

Transportation

Most Kenyans walk from place to place. In cities, people might take buses or taxis. People ride trains between large cities.

Famous Sight

People from all over the world come to see Kenya's wildlife. Visitors to Nairobi National Park look for lions, cheetahs, rhinos, giraffes, and zebras.

Country Facts

Name: Republic of Kenya

Capital: Nairobi

Population: 44,037,656 (July 2013 estimate)

Size: 224,962 square miles (582,649 square kilometers)

Languages: English, Kiswahili, other native languages

Main Crops: tea, coffee, corn, wheat, sugarcane, fruit

Money: Kenyan shilling

Kenya's flag

Critical Thinking Using the Common Core

1. Many Kenyan meals include corn. Name some ways in which corn is used. (Key Ideas and Details)

2. All kinds of wildlife live in Nairobi National Park. What might be some of the reasons they live there and not in the wild? (Integration of Knowledge and Ideas)